A CLASSIC BIBLE CHAPTER

EXODUS 20
The Ten Commandments

By

Allen C. Liles
Liles Communications, LLC

EXODUS 20
The Ten Commandments

by

Allen C. Liles
Liles Communications, LLC

Published By
Positive Imaging, LLC
bill@positive-imaging.com

ISBN: 9781951776510

This book is dedicated to my dear wife
and partner in ministry
Jan Carmen Liles

(1941-2017) RIP

Contents

INTRODUCTION

This is a book about God's Laws. It concerns one specific set of spiritual precepts (and perhaps the most famous)—The Ten Commandments. Here is a question for you: How relevant do you think these ancient Commandments are in today's 24/7 digital world? We already know that many people, especially in the 18-29 demographic group, are less religious and not prone to accept dogma in general. For the rest of us, it is doubtful that the most devout churchgoers could rattle off all 10 of God's primary Laws without pause. How important should they be in today's cancel culture? Are the Ten Commandments in need of deep revision because of technological changes? Personally, I stand with The Commandments. I believe these fundamental laws still have relevance and that present-day society may be undervaluing them. Just as they established standards for Jewish behavior thousands of years before Jesus Christ walked the earth, I believe these 10 rules for acceptable behavior are still pertinent. In fact, returning to the original Commandments might be crucial in reversing our moral decline. Are we trending downward in values and behavior? What do you think? Every relevant statistic shows crime of all kinds, divorce, drug addiction, pornography, gambling, alcoholism, suicide, mental illness, and increased use of profanity are all increasing. Rather than reversing themselves, these problems seem to be gaining momentum. Human beings are beautiful but imperfect creatures. We all have foibles and failings. Breaking God's (and society's) laws has become acceptable behavior. It is even encouraged and condoned by a permissive society. Unless this trend gets reversed, who knows where we might end up? Civil behavior might be irreparably damaged or even destroyed. We all know something is wrong. We need a moral reset to get centered again. Just as in Moses' day, people need eternal rules for basic human conduct. Perhaps we should remember the reason for the original Ten Commandments. God felt the Jewish people were lacking in two things: (1) spiritual direction and (2) personal discipline. God felt the freed slaves from Egypt could not enter the Promised Land without a basic Code of Conduct. The Jewish people needed reminding of how to honor God, their parents and each other. The same basic human need for direction and discipline still exists today. There is some good news regarding the Ten Commandments. With these 10 basic precepts long in place, we are not starting from zero. If followed, these timeless laws still promise hope

for a happier and more God-centered life.
Thousands of years after first being handed
off by God to Moses, the Commandments still
present a powerful and ordered way to
approach life. Another bit of good news: these
rules are already well known and accepted by
many. They are still revered and practiced
faithfully in some quarters. However, public
display of The Commandments still ignites
controversy. Some rue the mixing of church
and state. Yet, a majority of those polled are
not openly antagonistic toward The Commandments. This offers some hope and a
potential base for the reset of our moral com-
pass. It is generally true that God's rules suffer from inattention and neglect. Few spend
time worrying how their own behavior com-
pares to the original Commandments. A percentage of people probably follow these laws
because of their church-based upbringing and
long practiced personal values. However, not
many human beings arise each morning and
say: "Well I will break Commandments 1, 4
and 7 today. But I promise God to faithfully
keep 2, 3 and certainly number 6." Most people are far too busy living their daily lives to
constantly measure their spiritual behavior.
We do know that a moral crisis exists. To
retrieve our standards, a revolution might be
needed. A fresh look at the original Ten Commandments could be a part of that shift.

There was once a joke that, when Moses toted the two stone tablets down from Mount Sinai, many of the people became alarmed. There were just too many hard rules for such a rowdy and undisciplined group. Some urged their exalted leader to reduce the total number of Commandments to five or six manageable suggestions. Why did God feel the need for so many specific laws? Most likely, the Supreme Being had become tired of waiting for this Jewish clan to behave correctly on their own. The entire book of Exodus is filled with detailed and precise instructions regarding sacrifices and even building construction. In God's divine Mind, the Jewish people needed everything spelled out—and then some. Human conduct often cries out for rules and "boundaries". Has the world come full circle back to those ancient days? We are living in confused and troubled times. We worship countless idols other than God. Technology, money, fame, and power dominate our thoughts and actions. High profile social "Influencers" set our standards and parameters. We are told who to cancel and who we should revere. Old norms have been discarded. In many ways, we are a rudderless and fragile society. However, I think that many people still want divine guidance and moral principles from a source greater than themselves. Of all the "codes" and "rules" ever brought forth directly from God, the Ten Commandments remain the best and most durable. They should be restored to prominence. I believe we need these basic laws now more than ever. Without a doubt, they contain the wisdom and power to lead us back to a new morality. God knows we need it.

Rev Allen C. Liles
April, 2021

PREPARATION FOR STUDYING

THE TEN COMMANDMENTS

OPENING PRAYER

"Dear God, please open my heart, mind and spirit to your precepts and laws. We need your Ten Commandments now more than ever. Help me to set aside any precon-ceived notions or biases. Allow me to empty myself of all negativity. Let me receive your Holy Laws without any trace of resentment against religion or dogma. Assist me in recognizing the intrinsic value of sacred codes for behavior and conduct. Inscribe these words on the wisdom tablets of my heart: "Today, I will be open and receptive to the laws of God." Thank you, God. Amen and amen."

MEDITATION:

Find a quiet and familiar place where you can remain undisturbed for a minimum of 15 minutes. Sit with both feet flat on the floor. Place your hands in your lap with the palms turned upward. Now take a deep breath. Breathe in through your nose, until your lungs are filled with air. Hold that breath and count silently to yourself 1-2-3-

4-5. Now open your mouth wide and push the breath out, counting 1-2-3-4-5. Take one more deep breath and repeat the same process.

Now read these words: "God, I need your wisdom and guidance. I want your rules on how to live my life. Bless me with your divine Presence. Let it flow in and through my spirit at this very moment. I want to understand your laws and their place in my life. Please activate The Holy Spirit within me."

Close your eyes and sit in the silence for five full minutes. Try and empty your mind of all extraneous thoughts. Relax. Listen in the quietness for the still, small voice of God. Do not be concerned if nothing materializes. Just stay calm and serene for the entire five minutes. Have no expectations. Enjoy the stillness. At the end of the quiet time, you will have a degree of serenity even if chooses to remain silent. Come back and meditate at any time for whatever length and depth you require. Talk to God. No subject is off limits.

PRAYER OF THANKSGIVING
LORD, thank you for this peaceful time with you. I appreciate being with you in the quietness of meditation. It increases my sense of peacefulness and well-being. I need this time

apart with you. I want to understand your rules for human behavior. I know you love and cherish each one of your children. You want only the best for us. For that, I express my deepest gratitude. Thank you, thank you, thank you, God.

BIBLICAL TEXT

EXODUS 20: Verses 1 - 6

1—And God spoke all these words:
2—"I am the Lord your God, who brought
you out of Egypt, out of the land of slavery.
3—You shall have no other gods before me.
4—You shall not make for yourself an image
in the form of anything in heaven above or
on the earth beneath or in the waters below.
5—You shall not bow down to them or
worship them; for I, the LORD your God, am
a jealous God, punishing the children for the
sins of the parents to the third and fourth
generation of those who hate me,
6—but showing love to a thousand
generations of those who love me and keep
my commandments.

EXODUS 20: Verses 7 - 11

7—You shall not misuse the name of the
LORD your God, for the LORD will not hold
anyone guiltless who misuses his name.
8—Remember the Sabbath day by keeping it
holy
9—Six days you shall labor and do all your
work,
10—but the seventh day is a sabbath to the
LORD your God. On it you shall not do any

work, neither you nor your son or daughter, nor your male or female servant, nor your animals, nor any foreigner residing in your towns.

11—For in six days the LORD made the heavens and the earth, the sea and all that is in them, but he rested on the seventh day. Therefore, the LORD blessed the Sabbath day and made it holy.

EXODUS 20: Verses 12 - 13

12—Honor your father and your mother, so that you may live long in the land the LORD your God is giving you.

13—You shall not murder.

EXODUS 20: Verses14 - 15

14—You shall not commit adultery.

15—You shall not steal.

EXODUS 20: Verses 16 -17

16—You shall not give false testimony against your neighbor.

17···You shall not covet your neighbor's house. You shall not covet your neighbor's wife, or his male or female servant, his ox or donkey, or anything that belongs to your neighbor.

EXODUS 20: Verses 18 - 21

18—When the people saw the thunder and lightning and heard the trumpet and saw the mountain in smoke, they trembled with fear. They stayed at a distance

19—and said to Moses, "Speak to us yourself and we will listen. But do not have God speak to us or we will die."

20---Moses said to the people, "Do not be afraid. God has come to test you, so that the fear of God will be with you to keep you from sinning."

21---The people remained at a distance, while Moses approached the thick darkness where God was.

EXODUS 20: Verses 22 - 26

22---Then the LORD said to Moses, "Tell the Israelites this: "You have seen for yourselves that I have spoken to you from heaven.

23---Do not make any gods to be alongside me; do not make for yourselves gods of silver or gods of gold.

24---Make an altar of earth for Me and sacrifice on it your burnt offerings, your sheep and your goats and your cattle. Wherever I cause my name to be honored, I will come to you and bless you.

25—If you will make an altar of stones for me, do not build it with dressed stones, for you will defile it if you use a tool on it.

26—And do not go up to my altar on steps, or your private parts will be exposed."

OVERHEARD ON THE TOP OF MOUNT SINAI:

A CONVERSATION BETWEEN GOD AND MOSES

"Well, My LORD, that was some arrival!", Moses said with genuine awe in his voice. "What a showstopper!"

"Yes, I brought the thunder and lightning with Me this time," The Creator replied, "I wanted the people to know that it is indeed I, the Supreme Ruler of the entire universe. Better to start off with a bang rather than a whimper!"

"Oh, I do not think anyone will be confused," Moses smiled. "Most of the people are still quaking in their sandals at the foot of the mountain."

"Good," God laughed, "I do not want them approaching Me up here. If they do, I will have to break out against them."

"Yes, you were firm about that," Moses agreed, "I think they heard you loud and clear. Especially loud."

"Now, I want you to go back down and bring somebody up here with you next time. You will need extra help in carrying these two heavy stone tablets back down the mountain. Remember, Moses, you are over eighty years old. You could trip and fall. The sight of you tumbling head over heels down the mountain would not inspire confidence."

"Two stone tablets?" Moses asked, "Heavy, you say?"

"Yes," God answered. "They contain a number of My specific laws, ten in fact. I am calling them the Ten Commandments."

"10, did you say?", Moses said, sounding a bit perplexed.

"Why?" God responded. "Would you like more? I already have dozens of other requirements which you and I will discuss later. However, these Ten Commandments are the most important laws right now. They represent the specific ways that human beings should govern their behavior. This set of My sacred precepts is non-negotiable. However, do not fret. I have other requirements on everything from burnt offerings to construction projects. But we can visit later about those things. Right now, let you and I stay focused on these two stone tablets. I wrote them myself. Look, Mo, I have waited on the Jewish people to get their act together. It is not going to happen. I have had it up to here with their all too human behavior. They are a scraggly lot. Yes, I understand human beings and their weaknesses better than anyone. After all, I created every one of you. I love and cherish My precious children. I also realize that life can be confusing. I knew that you might not comprehend Free Will choice. Therefore, I have been patient. I kept hoping human beings would figure out how to behave on their own. After thousands of years, I have given up. I think you all need closer supervision. Hence, The Ten Commandments.'"

"Yes, Father," Moses said with a bow, "You are probably right about us. We can be slow learners. What would you have me do?"

"I want you to carry these two tablets down to the people," God told Moses. "Explain them all in detail. Field their questions if you must. But expect blowback, especially on the number of Commandments. People will want you to cut back the tablets from two to one. If you took a secret vote, they would probably eliminate the laws about adultery and coveting. Coveting is a hobby with these people. You might also be surprised about their reluctance to hold down the swearing and blasphemy. People love their expletives, even the women.

I get that aspect of human nature. It is also the reason I included cursing on My original list. I want people to be more careful about the way they talk. It is past time for them to clean up their act. We have too much trash talking. It does nothing to enhance discourse. Listening to them swear constantly is hard on My ears."

"No s---t!" Moses blurted out.

God laughed.

Moses was noticing that Spirit seemed to enjoy this back-and-forth informal banter. The shepherd had never really felt relaxed in God's divine Presence before. That thing at the burning bush still spooked him. But this was a friendly exchange, almost like chatting with an intimate pal.

"I know human nature," Moses ventured, "People do not like being told what to do. I suspect that dropping a couple of harsh sounding tablets on them will not change their attitude toward authority."

"I AM sure of it," God nodded. "However, I want you to stand your ground when the murmuring starts. Allow them to bicker among themselves. Just do not back off from the original 10 Commandments. I know these people. They are contentious. Arguing is second nature for them. They will whine, become angry and even try threatening you. Do not give them an inch. I will back you up, Moses. The Jewish people need these laws before they can enter the Promised Land."

"I agree they can be a rascally bunch," Moses agreed, "I hear their confounded murmuring every day. The worst of them will never murmur to my face, but I always hear about it later. It is the one thing I hate about leadership. Those at the top are always being questioned and discussed."

"How well I know," God nodded. "Put yourself in My place. The buck really does stop with Me. Everything gets piled up on My doorstep. However, I keep loving everybody, no matter what they say or do. I agree with you that being in charge is never easy. Human beings love disrespecting and ignoring their leaders. It makes them feel powerful. When that happens, I just love them a little more."

"That is why you are the Supreme Being and I am only a shepherd," Moses smiled, "Now I better go fetch somebody to give me a hand with these two tablets. I will be back soon. I also want to have a better look at those laws myself before the sun goes down. I promise not to murmur."

"Good man," God said, placing a hand on Moses' shoulder. "I AM really glad things worked out at the burning bush.," the Supreme Being smiled. "You should have seen that look on your face that day. Oh, how you protested! You told me: "You've got the wrong man. I am too old and decrepit. I stammer and cannot speak in front of people." Geez, how you protested. But everything worked out for the best. You have more than exceeded My expectations. Now get back down the mountain and fetch some help. It will be dark soon."

EXPANDED COMMENTARY

EXODUS 20: 1-6:

THE FIRST AND SECOND COMMANDMENTS

EXODUS 20: 1—And God spoke all these words:

It was important for the writer of Exodus (probably Moses) to establish that the Ten Commandments originated from God. No other source would have been acceptable to the Jewish people. The gravity of the specific laws required authentication from the ultimate authority.

EXODUS 20: 2—I am the LORD your God, who brought you out of Egypt, out of the land of slavery.

God wants to establish His identity and purpose. He also wants to remind the people what He has done for them. God has delivered the Jews from slavery to freedom. It was not an easy task. Many false hopes were dashed before freedom was finally granted.

God's involvement in the process represents an excellent reason for the Jewish people to pay attention. By also referring to Himself as "your God", the LORD sets the stage for the next verse.

THE FIRST COMMANDMENT: YOU SHALL HAVE NO OTHER GODS BEFORE ME

EXODUS 20: 3—You shall have no other Gods before me.

It could be argued that Exodus 20:3 is the key verse in this entire Classic Bible Chapter. Human beings continually set up idols and worship them before God. Perhaps part of this idol worship is that the "Real God" is invisible to the naked eye. Materially conceived gods can be viewed and experienced through the five senses. This gives them the credibility impossible for an immanent and transcendent God. The "Real God" is within us but also resides in the splendor of Heaven. In addition, some material "gods" can provide instant gratification. Drugs, alcohol, sex, gambling, fame, and power produce immediate pleasure and temporary happiness for many who are stuck in materiality. Given our impatient nature for satisfaction, It is easy to see how some idols qualify for human worship. Spiritual transformation is a long-term process. It takes hard work and often arrives in the dead of night. Probably no human action disturbs our "Real God" more than watching lesser gods being routinely placed ahead of Him. God has chosen this as the First Commandment for many reasons. Foremost is that, if people do not follow this specific law, then nothing else that follows matters.

THE SECOND COMMANDMENT: YOU SHALL MAKE NO FALSE IDOL

EXODUS 20:4—You shall not make for yourself an image in the form of anything in heaven above or on the earth beneath or in the waters below.

God understood that people love images. Most human beings are visual learners. They would choose a visual in-person experience over any other. You can read about a popular musical artist, watch a YouTube performance, and/or listen to their recordings. But seeing the artist perform in person brings everything together. God also realized that people enjoy rallying together for worship. "Gathering" in front of something tangible encourages human bonding and a sense of "family." Worshipping as part of a "crowd" could help affirm the idol's credibility for doubters. A spiritual God cannot be experienced by the five senses. Worshipping an unseen deity requires deep faith and unswerving belief. It takes conscious awareness of a hidden power greater than oneself. Understanding abstract concepts and ideas was not that common 5000 years ago. An actual "idol" was probably much easier to comprehend.

EXODUS 20: 5—You shall not bow down and worship them for I, the LORD your God, am a jealous God, punishing the children for the sins of the parents to the third and fourth generation of those who hate me.

God wants to make sure there is no misunderstanding about the negativity of idol worship. By saying that His punishment for such misbehavior will extend down through generations, God is putting people on notice. Idol worship is the ultimate red line for a jealous Deity. The LORD means business with His displeasure and the people best know it. The Creator of the universe will not be mocked.

EXODUS 20: 6----but showing love to a thousand generations of those who love me and keep My commandments.

God also offers the "carrot" of an extended and far greater blessing to those who put Him first. For the people who put God first before false gods and idols, they can expect rich rewards.

ADDITIONAL THOUGHTS ON EXODUS 20: VERSES 1-6.

The chapter begins after Moses has returned to the top of Mount Sinai (also known as Horeb) several times. Now God is ready to share the specific Ten Commandments. The LORD knew Moses would need help carrying the two stone tablets back down the mountain, so he requested that his brother Aaron assist him. Of course, Joshua (Moses' second in command) would have been a more likely candidate. However, he was at the foot of the mountain, helping people build an idol. It is doubtful that Joshua would have been thrilled with the 2nd Commandment. God had made it clear that the people should not attempt to come back up the mountain with Moses. The leader of the two million former slaves understood that God had "put limits around the mountain and put it apart as holy" (Exodus 19:23). It is interesting that God speaks of himself here in the third person: "But the priests and the people must not force their way through to come up to the LORD, or he will break out against them." (Exodus 19:21). Moses then descended Mount Sinai and repeated God's warning. It is not hard not to picture some murmuring among people at being excluded and told to keep their distance. One wonders how Moses really felt about these detailed laws. God begins by reminding the Jewish leader of who He is: "I am the LORD your God who brought you out of Egypt, out of the land of slavery." That had not been an easy process. The ruling Pharaoh had changed his mind several times about releasing the slaves. In return for the reluctance, God had foisted plagues, droughts, and assorted other problems on the Egyptian ruler to make him change his mind. After Pharaoh finally did let the slaves go, he then proceeded to chase after them with 600 chariots filled with his strongest warriors. He cornered the Israelis at the Red Sea. Only God parting the waters brought them to safety. Still, they had yet to enter the Promised Land. Moses would not live to see that glorious day. But without their blessed shepherd , it would have never happened.

EXODUS 20: 7-11

THE THIRD AND FOURTH COMMAND-MENTS

THE THIRD COMMANDMENT: YOU SHALL NOT TAKE GOD'S NAME IN VAIN

Exodus 20:7---You shall not misuse the name of the LORD your God, for the LORD will not hold anyone guiltless who misuses his name.

Some Bible versions read "Thou shalt not take the name of the LORD your God in vain" to describe this Commandment. The fact that God elevated a warning against blasphemy to #3 overall demonstrates its importance. This Commandment perhaps falls under the scope of the first two precepts as another form of human disrespect toward God. Putting "God" and "damn" together in one expression could be literally taken as "Damning God". Human beings are often not effective swearers anyway. Many of today's linguists believe the coarseness in society and an increased use of profanity are working together to debase our culture. It is hard not to agree.

Exodus 20:8-11

THE FOURTH COMMANDMENT: YOU SHALL KEEP THE SABBATH DAY HOLY

Verse 8: Remember the Sabbath by keeping it holy.

Verse 9: Six days you shall labor and do all the work.

Verse 10: but the seventh day is a sabbath to the LORD your God. On it you shall not do any work, neither you or your son or daugh-

ter, nor any male or female servant; nor any foreigner residing in your home.

Verse 11: For in six days the LORD made the heavens and the earth; but he rested on the seventh day. Then the LORD blessed the Sabbath day and made it holy.

Sabbaths vary. The Jewish faith and a few Christian movements recognize Saturday as the Sabbath. Most Protestant and Catholic congregations choose Sunday as the designated "day of rest and worship". Without question, this Commandment harkens back to God's creation of the world. The LORD rested on the seventh day of that process. A complementary belief is that God wanted to make sure people put aside at least one day each week to grow spiritually. Of course, the custom of having a holy sabbath universally observed by one and all has vanished. Retail stores, once closed on Sundays, now remain open 24/7 to serve their customers and increase profits. One wonders how God regards this deviation from the 4th Commandment. It could be interpreted as still another example of disrespect toward the Creator. No one expects the current retail store policies to change. Of course, people can still choose any day of the week to further their spiritual growth. A customized Sabbath would probably be accepted by a forward-thinking God.

Holiness can indeed occur anytime and any-
place. The main goal of this Commandment
is to rest from your labors while honoring
God.

EXODUS 20: 12-13

THE FIFTH AND SIXTH COMMAND-
MENTS

THE FIFTH COMMANDMENT:
HONOR YOUR FATHER AND MOTHER

**Exodus 20:12—Honor your father and
mother, so that you may live long in the land
the LORD your God is giving you.**

Family is always important, whether in Bib-
lical days or today. Families can be the
source of joyful and fulfilling moments. But it
can also produce conflict and pain. Many
family relationships suffer from a lack of
respect by children toward their parents.
Parent/child interaction provides a frame-
work for both positive and negative out-
comes. At some point, children seek to assert
their own independence. Parents, by their
nature, are protectors, advisors, guidance
counselors and dispensers of wisdom and jus-
tice. An eventual clash is inevitable. Angry
words and actions can be devastating for
both sides. Disrespectful comments between

a parent and child can be irretrievable. A fractious split often lasts a lifetime. In this Commandment, God adds an interesting "carrot" for the children. If they will honor their father and mother, it could ensure them of a long life. In this Commandment, God seems to take the side of parents. But there are no perfect parents, just as there are no perfect children. Some fathers and mothers have little or no parenting skills. Their own irresponsible behavior can endanger the child. Just because a parent may be taller and older, that does mean they possess the basic skills to do a good or even passable job. Many children are wise beyond their parent's years. Still, in this important precept, God takes the side of parents. In the New Testament (Ephesians 6:4, the Apostle Paul urges fathers not to exasperate their children. There are many negative parent/child relationships where blame can be applied to both sides. Hopefully, time will heal all wounds and parents and children will mature and grow. So much is gained when forgiveness and understanding are applied. A respectful and honoring relationship between parent and child can sow beautiful seeds of gratitude, appreciation and love.

THE SIXTH COMMANDMENT: YOU SHALL NOT MURDER

EXODUS 20: 13—You Shall Not Murder

God created humankind. Therefore, He understands the complexity of human nature. Each person is capable of love and generosity one minute and then anger and murderous resentment the next. An all-seeing God witnesses daily examples of man's inhumanity to man. At any level of consciousness, human beings are capable of dangerous emotions. Taking the life of another person can never be condoned as a rational act. However, for an individual prone to violence, a confrontation resulting in someone's death might seem like a normal outcome. "He (or she) deserved it!" or "They were asking for it", some murderers might say after taking a human life. In this Commandment, God is telling us that murder is always wrong. Ramping down emotions before violence happens becomes a necessity. Feelings must never escalate to murderous actions. What about self-defense as a justification for murder? God does not include any caveat, even to preserve one's own life. One secret to complying with this Commandment lies in society not tacitly giving permission to commit violence against someone else. When a commitment to non-violence becomes embedded in the popular culture, murders should become much rarer. As people begin to regard their neighbor as themselves, doing harm to others will be viewed as unthinkable. Although God seems to reference physical murder with this Commandment, people often "murder" each other both verbally and emotionally. For the victim, getting "killed" by verbal abuse can feel exactly like being physically murdered. No person should inflict damage of any kind on a fellow human being. With this Commandment, God seeks to take physical violence off the table.

EXODUS 20: 14-15

THE SEVENTH AND EIGHTH COMMANDMENTS

THE SEVENTH COMMANDMENT: YOU SHALL NOT COMMIT ADULTERY

EXODUS 20: 14—YOU SHALL NOT COMMIT ADULTERY

Sexual infidelity represents an area of great conflict between individuals. An unfaithful spouse can rupture any long-term commitment. In some cases, an emotional affair may be just as deadly as a physical breach of trust. How literal is God being with this Commandment? Does adultery begin with the first flirtation? Can you have "lust in the heart" without breaking this Commandment? Does being attracted to a co-worker threaten your marital relationship or commitment to a significant other? What comes first with adultery? Is it thoughts, feelings or actions? The mind must obviously get involved before the body can proceed to act in an adulterous manner. A conscious decision must first be made in someone's brain to dishonor marital vows. God understands the mysteries of human nature. Rationalization of certain behavior can also play a role in the consummation of adultery. "I deserve to have an affair," one party might say or "Look at what I have to put up with at home." Another person might justify their actions this way: "You drove me to it" or "I have to get my needs met." Human beings are adept at rationalizing anything, especially where sex is involved. Adultery can be triggered by opposite feelings like boredom and anger. In many ways, the human ego often encourages infidelity. Habit is another trigger, along with family of origin factors. "My dad was a ladies' man," one wayward son might argue, "It is in my genes." A female voice might counter with "My mother was married six times. One man couldn't satisfy her." With the Seventh Commandment, God is addressing the true boundaries of human behavior. Honoring a commitment when temptation beckons can be the ultimate litmus test for any relationship. Adultery is an enormous factor in the soaring divorce rate. God seems to understand the importance of fidelity, hence a specific Commandment to address the problem. The question is how many people will consider this moral law before being unfaithful. At least, God is on record as to where She stands.

THE EIGHTH COMMANDMENT: YOU SHALL NOT STEAL

EXODUS 20: 15—YOU SHALL NOT STEAL

Stealing takes many forms. In the case of the Eighth Commandment, God seems to mean the theft of physical property. Taking someone else's possessions is a criminal act. Society uses specific laws to impose penalties upon those who dare steal somebody's "stuff". It extracts time, money and freedom from convicted thieves. "Don't do the crime unless you can do the time" is a well-known warning statement. God reaffirms this response from society by canonizing it through this Commandment. Stealing from another person can often be a crime of opportunity. Car keys are left in the ignition. A glass sliding door remains invitingly open. A delivered package goes unattended on the front porch. A garage door is up, exposing a vehicle or other valuable property. Somebody walks along a city street, not paying attention to their surroundings. A bicycle is left unsecured, making it a tempting target. Someone stuffs their billfold with cash from an ATM without understanding their potential as a robbery victim. On and on it goes. These daily occurrences show the many and varied temptations available to anyone who would steal. Again, God understands human nature. By making specific reference to not stealing, Spirit wants people to understand that theft is not acceptable. Hopefully, this Commandment might cause a potential criminal to think twice before deciding to become a thief. Knowing human beings as He does, God wants to discourage criminal behavior. Preventing a costly mistake before it happens could be another motivation. Getting caught and being convicted of stealing can ruin someone's life. God is always caring, forgiving and concerned about the welfare of Her precious children. Stopping a crime before it occurs committed shows Spirit's kindness and concern for everyone, both perpetrator and victim. Yet, if someone decides to proceed with becoming a thief, God could rightfully remind us: "I warned you."

EXODUS 20: 16-17

THE NINTH AND TENTH COMMANDMENT

THE NINTH COMMANDMENT: YOU SHALL TELL LIES ABOUT YOUR NEIGHBOR

EXODUS 20: 16—YOU SHALL NOT BEAR FALSE TESTIMONY AGAINST YOUR NEIGHBOR

Why do human beings tell lies about each other? Gossip, slander and negative comments have one common motive. It is to take others down while puffing yourself up. If you can succeed in lowering another's status, then perhaps people will think better of you. For the purveyor of the lie, it almost never works. For starters, be assured that whatever you say about someone else will get back to them. If you do not care about creating a life-long enemy, then proceed to distribute your lie. However, few personal choices backfire so quickly on the perpetrator than bearing false witness against somebody else. This act always speaks loudest on the liar's integrity and worth. Some lies manage to live on for a while. Eventually, the truth washes up on the shores of time. The Ninth Commandment addresses a subtle crime that never pays off for anyone. God realizes the damage that lies can inflict. Some foolish people resort to lying even when the truth might be easier. Lying can become habitual and a default way to handle one's life. Gossip is a serial killer, randomly assaulting reputations. Personal slander is a higher form of gossip, often reckless in the extreme. Once you are branded as someone who "carries tales", prepare for a lonely life. Friends do not tear each other down. They are the builders of reputations. Spreading falsehoods is akin to littering the neighborhood with garbage. God wants His children to get along with one another. Bearing false witness is guaranteed to fracture even the most solid of relationships. This is a Commandment worthy of strict attention. There are no harmless lies, only harmful consequences. God is telling us to think twice before violating this Commandment. Words are like bullets. Once fired, they cannot be retrieved. Consciously choose not to lie about someone else. It can be one of the wisest decisions you will ever make.

THE TENTH COMMANDMENT: YOU SHALL NOT WANT YOUR NEIGHBOR'S THINGS

EXODUS 20:17----THOU SHALL NOT COVET YOUR NEIGHBOR'S HOUSE. YOU SHALL NOT COVET YOUR NEIGHBOR'S WIFE, OR HIS MALE OR FEMALE SERVANT, HIS OX OR DONKEY, OR ANYTHING THAT BELONGS TO YOUR NEIGHBOR.

Almost everybody has wanted someone else's home, relationships, family status, financial well-being, automobile, clothes, vacation trips, job position, handsomeness, beauty, physical endowments, athletic ability or a million other things. Why do we engage in such a waste of time? In a few cases that often end up on crime TV, people act out their fantasies. They construct elaborate plots to seize the asset in question. It never ends well. God understands how the human brain often lives in a "The grass is always greener" state of mind. However, this mentality resembles being stuck in neck-deep quicksand. Once you begin the habit of coveting, it becomes hard to stop. The coveter rarely appreciates his or her own blessings. The thing you covet may not be what you think. That fancy car can get repossessed by the bank tomorrow. Your girlfriend's handsome new boyfriend may have a huge gambling problem. The beautiful mansion can be drowning in toxic mold. Your roommate's glitzy new job can be eliminated overnight. A famous songstress once sang "It's not having what you want, it's wanting what you have." People can project themselves into the wildest imagining. Appreciate what you have. It can be far more precious than anything you might covet. Pay attention to this important Commandment and God's eternal wisdom. He wants to save you from coveting, a waste of time.

OTHER VERSES

EXODUS 20:18-26

EXODUS 20: 18—When the people saw the thunder and lightning and heard the trumpet and saw the mountain in smoke, they trembled with fear. They stayed at a distance.

EXODUS 20: 19—and said to Moses, "Speak to us yourself and we will listen. But do not have God to speak to us or we will die."

EXODUS 20:20—Moses said to the people, "Do not be afraid. God has come to test you, so that the fear of God will be with you to keep you from sinning."

EXODUS 20:21—The people remained at a distance, while Moses approached the thick darkness where God was.

I am sure you have heard or used the phrase: "He (or she) put the fear of God in me." In this four-verse sequence, it is clear what God meant to accomplish. He wanted to create genuine fear in the people. God was about to present strict new laws that the former slaves were to live by. The LORD needed for them to pay attention. These Ten Commandments were serious business. There is no

meekness whatsoever with this powerful and
thundering God. Perhaps Spirit added the
lightning and thunder for effect. However, He
wanted them to understand that a mighty
God was in their midst. It worked. The people
were afraid to approach this powerful Spirit,
lest it cost them their lives. Even though
Moses explained that this noisy and bluster-
ing God was only testing them, the people
appear reluctant to take a chance. The former
slaves appear content to have their leader
(Moses) act as the go-between.

EXODUS 20: 22-26

EXODUS 20:22—Then the LORD said to
Moses, "Tell the Israelites this: "You have
seen for yourself that I have spoken to you
from heaven.

EXODUS 20:23—Do not make any Gods to be
alongside me; do not make for yourselves gods
of silver or gods of gold.

EXODUS 20:24—Make an altar of earth for
me and sacrifice on it your burnt offerings,
your sheep and your goats and your cattle.
Wherever I cause my name to be honored, I
will come to you and bless you.

EXODUS 20:25—If you will make an altar of stones for me, do not build it with dressed stones, for you will defile it if you use a tool on it.

EXODUS 20:26—And do not go up to my altar on steps, or your private parts will be exposed."

The LORD is making clear His wishes regarding altars and sacrifices. The specific instructions seem firm and non-negotiable. This is yet another example of how God wants the people to obey Him. One senses that Spirit has become frustrated after being ignored and disrespected. He brought the Jewish people out of slavery. He made freedom a reality. Yet, it seems that God still wants proof that the people will follow His dictates. He obviously doubts their obedience and commitment. Remember, even when Moses was meeting with God on the mountain, the people below were busy building another idol. There is little doubt that God's thundering persona has gotten their attention. Yet it remains unclear if they will follow His instruction. That verse about protecting their private parts is somewhat curious, except to say that God observes everything. Moses must play a crucial role in convincing the Jewish people of God's seriousness. He obviously fears the LORD, but he has also

experienced the wishy-washiness of those
under his leadership. Many trials still lie
ahead for everyone. Moses understands that
deliverance remains uncertain. They are still
a long way from the Promised Land.

TEN COMMANDMENT STORIES

THE FIRST COMMANDMENT:

YOU SHALL HAVE NO OTHER GODS BEFORE ME

Lance Rainier could not believe his good fortune. Lisa, his new girlfriend of five days, had a rich father who loved spoiling his only daughter. Anything Lisa wanted was fine with daddy. After a wild night at her luxury condo on the beach, Lisa had suggested they head for the airport and fly to Acapulco for a few days. Since Lance had long since maxxed out his last remaining credit card, he had no personal means to oblige her.

"Er, I'm not sure that's a good idea," he told Lisa, "I'm a little short on cash right now." Lance was in his mid-20s. He was still collecting a weekly unemployment check after being fired from the bait shop located a block off the beach. Although underfunded, he was long on the kind of good looks the bikini girls liked. Lance was able to romance a different girl every night and often did. If they did not insist on him spending money, things went well. When a girl became demanding about anything, it was goodbye Lance. Since he had renounced social media some months ago, it was hard for the disgruntled women to track him down.

Lance had lured Lisa in without exerting much effort. Since then, the duo had become inseparable. The Acapulco trip might be the first test of their relationship, he thought. When Lance mentioned he was part of the cashless society, Lisa had visibly frowned and responded with two words: "Oh really?"
"I don't suppose your dad would stake us," Lance grinned, "would he?"

"My dad has a place right on the bay, lover boy." Lisa smiled, "And his private jet will take us down there. What is it that you need money for? I am buying. You are along for the ride. Lie back and enjoy it."

Lance had dated a few well-off girls during his time of trolling the beach, but Lisa was on a different level. She oozed wealth. It was his dream fantasy. She had found his sweet spot. Lance idolized and loved money. That was a bit strange, considering how little of it he possessed. Oh well, he thought, like the lady said: "I should just lie back and enjoy the ride."

Lance had not been raised in wealth, or any-thing close to it. His father was in his late-50s and a longtime assistant minister in a church that had been losing congregants every year. Lance's mother worked in the produce depart-ment at a chain grocery store. Together there was barely enough to feed the parents, Lance and his younger brother Thomas. Ten years ago, his father had developed serious vision problems with both eyes. He became legally blind before anything could be done to repair his eyesight. The church board voted to keep Lance's father employed part-time, mainly through the generosity of an older lady who felt sorry for the family. However, the board did cut his salary by half, thus straining the family budget even more. Lance knew that he should find a decent job and help the family more. However, he had to face facts. Being a slacker and persistent pothead, he had zero motivation and ambition.

The job at the bait shop was a perfect fit for Lance's low aspirations. He could donate a few dollars to the family stash now and then, while enjoying perfect access to the beach bunnies and his beloved pot. It really helped when his girlfriends had access to cash. If they were loaded with material goodies like a generous credit card and nice car, so much the better. After a while, most of the young women figured out that Lance was indeed a

leech and released him. Lisa, however, was
still in the pre-release mode. So far, so good,
Lance thought.

His assistant minister father had conversed
with him a couple of times about God. Once,
the dad asked his son if he was familiar with
the Ten Commandments. What a strange
question, Lance thought, He did remember
the first Commandment: something about not
having any other gods before Him. Lance wondered what God meant by that comment, but
he never asked his dad to explain it. Lance
usually found a cool way to distance himself
from any lengthy theology discussions with
his father. The family poverty was a sign that
God did not want His ministers to have any
ready cash. Lance would usually go outside
after any God-talk with his father and burn a
little weed. It settled him down. Then it was
back to the beach and chasing rich women.
That prospect appealed to him more than anything else in his non-descript life. And, he was
good at it.

Lance heard his cell beep. A text from Lisa
was coming in. It read "Where u? Plane ready.
Get with it, man! Now!" Lance stared at his
phone. However, he did not immediately text
her back. Why am I hesitating, he wondered.
He was getting a strange vibration, almost
like a red warning flag. The back of his neck

was tingling. This was not like him, hanging
back from a freebie weekend in Mexico with a
rich baby doll. He looked down at his cell and
saw his fingers moving. He had no idea what
he saying back to Lisa. As he hit "send", he
looked down and saw this message: "Can't
make it. Something came up. Have fun! C U!"
Within a few seconds, Lisa had responded
angrily with a "F U dummy" Well, so much for
that budding romance, he sighed.

The very next day, Lance could not miss the
front-page story: "Four local people killed as
private jet slams into mountain in Mexico."
He recognized Lisa's name. There were also
two pilots and one other man, aged 25 on
board the doomed plane. Lance kept staring
at the story for a few minutes. His hands were
shaking. Then, he rushed straight home.
"Where's Dad?" Lance asked his mother. "I
need to ask him a question about how God
works."

THE SECOND COMMANDMENT:

YOU SHALL NOT MAKE OR WORSHIP FALSE IDOLS

It was love at first sight for Allison Carroll, a
sophomore at Killeen High School in central
Texas. She had never seen or known anyone
like Tommy Franklin. He was a big-time

senior, co-captain and quarterback for a stud football team that had made it to the state semi-finals in the fall. On top of all that, Tommy was tall, dark, handsome and an approachable nice guy. Allison was sure he had never noticed her before that January 15 morning in the hallway outside the assistant principal's office. Tommy was just emerging from a meeting with Mr. Witmer, who was #2 in command at the high school. Allison was there to drop off a potted plant that had been delivered by mistake to Mrs. Jones, her home-room teacher. Allison never forgot what she had been wearing that day: a bright, yellow dress. The flowers in the potted plant were also golden in color.

Tommy's blue eyes took in all the colors and then noticed Allison's long blonde hair. He stepped back to size her up, then grinned and commented "Well, aren't you a breath of spring in the middle of winter?" Allison tried to respond, but her heart had already leaped straight to her throat. She could only smile weakly and nod her head affirmatively. Tommy was accustomed to having that effect on his fellow students, especially the younger girls. He stuck out his hand and smiled. "I'm Tommy," he said amicably. Allison was still operating in a semi-frozen state. However, she did manage to meekly return his friendly handshake. "I know," she managed, "I'm Allison Carroll." "Hi Allison Carroll," Tommy said, "Are you a sophomore or junior? You could not be a senior because I would have noticed you before now." Allison received a sudden jolt of confidence. She threw her head back and said, "Nope, I'm just a sophomore. Nobody notices us."

"Well, I'm noticing you now," Tommy said, "What are you doing after school?" Allison's new-found confidence fled immediately. "Er, I don't know," she responded, "Why?"

"Well, I'm meeting a couple of my buds for a burger. Would you want to join us? No pressure. Do your folks pick you up after school or do you ride the bus?"

"Bus," Allison said, still trying to process the conversation.

"Well, if you can clear it with your folks, I can take you home. You should be there before dark. Listen, just let me know before school is out. I will give you my cell. Text me where you want to meet."

Of course, Allison accepted his offer and sent the text. As they drove away from the school that afternoon in his cool BMW, she could sense the entire school watching them depart. It made her feel lightheaded. She experienced a contact high, just being in this wonderful man's presence. Allison suddenly felt older and more worldly. When Tommy fetched a pack of cigarettes out of his jacket pocket and casually lit one, he seemed like a full-grown man.

"Do you smoke?" he asked, thrusting the open pack toward her.

"Just once or twice," Allison responded, silently cursing her lack of sophistication. "Be my guest," Tommy insisted, shaking the pack so part of a cigarette popped up. She hesitated for a scant second, then reached over and secured it. Tommy flashed a smile and produced a lighter to complete the process. Allison took one drag and immediately began coughing. No instant worldliness today, she thought. Just then her cell beeped. Uh-oh. It was "Mom". At least she was not on Facetime. "Hi", she managed, finally getting her cough under control.

"Where are you?" Her mother asked, "You weren't on the bus." Her mom rarely waited at the stop or even noticed what time the bus arrived. After all, her daughter was 16.

"A friend is bringing me home today," Allison managed. She did not know what to do with the cigarette. It was developing a long ash already.

Tommy noticed her distress and motioned for her to hand him the cigarette.

What a great guy, she thought!

"Which friend?", her mom inquired.

"You haven't met him yet, "Allison said in a strange, but confident voice. "I will tell you all about it when I see you. Got to go. Sorry. Bye."

"That was mom," she explained.

"Yeah," Tommy said with a curious frown, "I gathered."

A couple of the football team's offensive line-man were waiting for the pair at the burger place. They were huge guys, but the four managed to squeeze in a booth without having to pull up a chair. Allison was the only girl. It made her feel tiny, but protected, being with such physically large men.

Everyone seemed to accept Allison's presence as the most natural thing in the world. One of the boys knew Sam, her older brother, who had graduated from high school the year before.

"What's he doing now?" the boy asked.

"He joined the Marines," she grimaced. "Can you believe it? He did his basic training in North Carolina. He's doing some other stuff now in San Diego."

All three boys shook their heads and laughed. "Not for me," Tommy said. "Thank God, I'm playing football in college. It pays better than the military."

The thought of him leaving town after high school never crossed Allison's mind.

"Sure, of course," she said, "Where?"

"Whoever pays the best," Tommy grinned. The other two boys shook their heads and laughed. "If you go to A & M, I'm going to kick your butt," one of them said.

The hour and fifteen minutes at the burger joint went by much too fast for Allison. She had barely spoken during the meal. Nobody had asked her a single question. Tommy had turned and smiled at her twice. Her heart had fluttered both times. She could feel something good happening between them.

"I better get you home," Tommy said. "Your mom might start worrying about you."

When Allison walked in her front door, she saw her mother staring out the window.

"Who was that?" She inquired. "I don't remember seeing that car before."

Allison kept moving toward her bedroom.

"Oh, nobody", she answered. Thankfully, her mom did not pursue the questioning. At least not for now.

Allison knew what she had to do. Her shrine to Tommy Franklin began that night. She found an old football program with his picture and cut it out. Allison expunged a meaningless photograph taken with her friends from an old frame and substituted Tommy's picture. She rummaged through her drawers until she found an unused candle. It was lit and placed next to the newly framed photograph. Allison then went to the laptop and Googled her hero. She printed off a couple of complimentary stories about Tommy's football exploits. She used them to start a "Tommy Franklin" scrapbook. Within half an hour, a mini shrine had been constructed. Then Allison climbed into her bed and visualized Tommy lying next to her. She slept soundly that night, a more peaceful sleep than she could ever remember. Her life had changed forever.

Allison checked her phone for any texts from Tommy the next morning, but nothing had arrived. There was no "How r u this morn‐ing?" Or "Had great time yesterday! U?" At school, her eyes searched for him. She walked by his locker twice, which was out of the way for her. Still nothing. Neither did she encoun‐ter the other two jocks that had shared the meal with them. It was as if Tommy and his friends had vanished from the face of the earth.

That night, Allison added a few more items to her Tommy Shrine. She had stenciled out the name "TOMMY" in art class and then tacked it on the wall next to her mirror. As she pre‐pared for bed, a thought crossed her mind. Should she text him? However, she resisted the urge.

At school the next day, there was still no Tommy. She casually asked Barb, her closet friend, if she had seen him. "You mean Tommy Franklin, the quarterback?" Barb had asked inquisitively. "Why?" she added. Allison shared the news about their burger date. "Oh, really?" Barb had commented, almost wide‐eyed. Her sophomore best friend having a date with the school's football captain! That was big-time news.

Once again, Allison patrolled by Tommy's locker with no sightings. After returning home from school, she decided to take the plunge and text him. Allison waited with her phone in hand for the next 20 minutes, but there was no response. Then she checked the phone every 15 minutes or so until it was time for bed. Tommy never answered her text. She finally decided to watch the 10 p.m. local newscast with her mom before heading to bed. In the sports segment, the newscaster had an excited announcement. A certain local high school quarterback had just signed a letter of intent to attend the University of Georgia in Athens, Georgia. Tommy was shown with the Bulldogs' head coach at a news conference in the Peach state. Standing behind Tommy at the signing table was his mother, father and some blonde girl. She was identified as the quarterback's steady girlfriend. Allison could not believe her eyes. She did not say anything to her mom, except to quickly excuse herself. Allison needed to get upstairs right away. She had some important work to do. The Tommy shrine had to go.

THE THIRD COMMANDMENT:

YOU SHALL NOT TAKE GOD'S NAME IN VAIN

The three job applicants sat in the waiting room of the retail store's personnel office. Their names were Jed, Teddy and Freddie. Jed was 22, Teddy had just turned 21 and Freddie was a young woman of 19.

"Man, is it f-----g hot out there today!" Freddie offered.

"G-----n right!" Teddy agreed.

"No s---t," Jed chimed in.

"Are we all three applying for the same f-----g job?" Freddie asked.

"How the s---t should I know? Teddy answered, "My dad told me the f-----s were hiring and to get my sorry a—down here ASAP."

"My parole officer sent me," Jed added. The a-----e knows some d-------d in the personnel office. I forgot the m-----------s name."

"I don't have any f-----g skills," Freddie announced. "I dropped out of high school last year before I graduated. I don't need any g----

m piece of paper to tell me I'm hot s—t. Pretty soon, the whole f------g world will know it."
"Well, I made it out of high school by the skin of my f------g teeth, "Teddy said, "I thought I might have to give the principal a b---j-b to get my diploma. WTF! What a b-----d. I would still like to kick his g----m a--.

"Yeah, my principal was a major b---h", Jed swore. "If I ever see her sorry a—again, I'll slap the c--p out of her!"

"G----m straight!" Jed laughed.

Just then, the store's personnel manager appeared in the doorway. He was a young man in his early 30s, He held a sheaf of papers. "Which one of you g-----m m--------s wants to go first?" the man asked with a smile.

THE FOURTH COMMANDMENT:

REMEMBER THE SABBATH DAY AND KEEP IT HOLY

Dwayne Nielsen was an entrepreneur's entrepreneur. He lived to work and worked to live. He had started his grocery chain with one small store in the Twin Cities suburb of Burnsville, 15 miles south of Minneapolis. Within a dozen years, he had expanded north

to Anoka and east to Oakdale. Now, he was
planning his biggest store yet in Eden Prairie,
southwest of downtown. Other local grocery
chains like Lund's and Byerly's and Cub were
now taking him seriously. Dwayne was a definite contender.

There was just one small problem. Dwayne
was a getting a reputation as a stern and
demanding taskmaster of a boss. Personnel
turnover was spiking. His micromanaging and
workaholic tendencies had already cost him
two marriages. "You're never home anymore,"
his first wife Cheryl had told him as she
departed with their two teenage boys for
Naples, Florida. "Oh well, I knew what you
were when I married you," second wife Pat
had sighed. She had been his trusted secretary for seven years when Dwayne was putting together his empire. He proposed to Pat
two months after his divorce from Cheryl
became final. Dwayne and Pat tried working
together at the company for nearly two years,
but things had changed. She relocated to
Sedona, Arizona with a comfortable severance
package, both as a long-time employee and
short-term wife.

After the divorce from his second wife,
Dwayne just seemed to work harder. He tried
to trim his hours, but in truth nothing interested him besides work. Dwayne had no hob-

bies. He tried golf once. He shot 88, but that was just on the front nine. He never played again. One of his high school friends tried to get him interested in the Vikings, but Sunday was his favorite workday. There was just something about the sabbath, with all the customers and their families flowing through the stores all relaxed and with more time on their hands.

One Sunday, Dwayne slipped down to the produce department in the original Burnsville store. He enjoyed sorting out the offerings and making sure the fruits and vegetables were stocked and fresh. He was working the apples when a stranger approached him. The customer was in his late 50s or early 60s. He had long gray hair, and a pony-tail secured with a rubber band. Dwayne thought he looked a little rough but also sort of familiar.

"Do I know you?" he half-smiled at the man. "Actually, you do," the man half-smiled, "My brother is Bob Salman. He used to work for you, maybe five years ago."

"Yes, I remember Bob," Dwayne replied. "What is he doing now? I seem to recall him wanting a slower pace. We work pretty hard around here."

"He went over to Wal-Mart as a greeter," the man grinned. "He told me he loves it. He does not have to work on Sundays anymore. He also found a great church. He even sings in the choir. Bass."

"Good for him," Dwayne said. "What do you do?"

"I'm in apples," the man said, "I work over at the "U". We develop new apples. It's a fun job."

"Really?" Dwayne said, evidencing some interest. He loved apples and fancied himself an apple connoisseur. "I've always wanted to know more about what the "U" does there. Do they give tours?"

"Absolutely" the man answered. "By the way, I'm Andy Salman."

Dwayne held out his hand and they exchanged a friendly shake.

"What's the most interesting thing to know about apples?" the grocer asked.

"Oh, all sorts of things," Andy smiled. "Did you know that China is the number one apple producer in the world?"

"No, I didn't," Dwayne said. "What else?"

"Well, you probably know that apples come in three colors," Andy said, "Yellow, green and red. It also takes four to five years before an apple tree starts to produce any fruit. Did you know that apples were around 6,500 years before Jesus walked the earth? They are an old fruit."

"Say, did your brother have anything to say about working for me?" Dwayne inquired, "I would like to know."

"Do you want me to tell you the truth or should I lie to you?" Andy grinned. "Yeah, he had a lot to say. He told me that you only required your employees to work half a day and you didn't care which half it was."

"That's funny," Dwayne said, with an unconvincing smile. "I guess I am a tough boss. That is how I became successful. I expect results. You got to keep charging ahead. Are you charging ahead, Andy?"

"Nope, not really," the pony tailed man answered. "I guess I am kind of like that old apple tree. It takes me a while to settle in and start producing."

"Well, you would not do too well working for me," Dwayne said. "I need results now. You know, like today. It is all about the bottom line. You have to keep moving fast or they start gaining on you."

"Do you ever take a Sunday off?" Andy inquired.

"Oh, hell no," Dwayne replied. "That is my favorite day of the week," Dwayne responded. "Why do you ask?"

"Well, the U has started offering apple tasting classes. However, it only meets on Sundays. They really make a day out of it. The people who attend get to sample our test apples and give their opinions. It has become like a holy day for most of the people. They say it reminds them of worshipping at their own special church. Some of them refer to it as the "Apple Sabbath". We even serve a little communion wine to lighten things up. One of the regular attendees is even a retired priest. Half-way through the day, he gives a little homily about God, apples, or sometimes both. It is kind of neat."

"Where do I sign up?" Dwayne asked, "That's my kind of church."

"At least it will get you out of the store," Andy laughed, "You'll meet some nice people too. Wake up, Dwayne. There is a whole new world out there."

THE FIFTH COMMANDMENT:

HONOR YOUR FATHER AND MOTHER

Katharine Tracy idolized her father Frank. The two were alike in so many ways. Both were big personalities who lit up any room they entered. Frank Tracy was a natural politician. He never much aspired to anything higher than local politics, but he easily won six consecutive terms as mayor of their medium size city of Raytown, Missouri. Located a few miles east of Kansas City, Raytown was sort of a middling and nondescript place. However, it did get some attention from folks running for Congress and the U. S. Senate. And, of course, President Harry S Truman was from down the way in Independence. Old Harry had died in 1972, well before Katharine was born. Frank had met the former president once when he was a teenager in the Missouri delegation at Boys State. He was impressed and the experience triggered a lifelong interest in politics.

Katharine's mother was the exact opposite from her outgoing husband. Edith Tracy was stunningly quiet for a politician's wife. She had received her accounting degree from the state university in Columbia and then settled into the back office at her father's Chevrolet dealership. Frank came in one day looking for a Silverado truck. He picked one out and quiet Edith had helped finalize the paperwork. They were instantly drawn to each other, like two puzzle pieces fitting together. In any conversation, it was 98% Frank and 2% Edith, if that much. Frank barely took a breath as he held forth. You usually had to ask Edith a direct question to get a response. Yet, she was well liked by everyone that knew her and especially over at the First Baptist Church. She had helped the church's regular bookkeeper set up her books. Edith was sweet in that way.

Katharine was a superstar at Raytown Senior High School. She was a Bluejays cheerleader for three years and Queen of Sports her senior year. She graduated as the school's salutatorian, one tenth of a percentage point behind Martin Lamb King, Jr. who subsequently won a scholarship to Harvard. During her junior and senior years, Katharine served as the editor for the high school newspaper. She was an outspoken firebrand who spent many afternoons debating Dr. Markle, the high school principal. She even won some of the arguments.

The power of Katharine's personality had also extended to her college career at Mizzou U. She served on the college council all four years at the school, as president of her Zeta Tau Alpha sorority and as student body president during her senior year. She majored in broadcast journalism and worked at the campus radio station. When the chance came along after graduation to work in Sen. Blount's office in Washington, she grabbed it. The four years she served on the senator"s staff made her decide to run for political office at some point. She returned to Raytown and began a career in the newsroom at Channel 5, the CBS affiliate in Kansas City. She quickly landed the noon news anchor job. A few short years later, the local congressman from Raytown got himself indicted and Katharine decided to go after his seat. She was 33 years old when she was won 58% per cent of the special election vote. Now, Katharine Tracy was realizing her dreams. She was a happy girl and not even tied down romantically. However, the relationship with her parents was a paradox. She and her mother Edith barely spoke. Yet, she and Frank had grown even closer as she advanced politically. That was fine with Katharine. In truth, she often wondered if any man could ever displace her dad as the #1 man in her life.

Of course, Frank Tracy loved every minute of his daughter's professional and political ascent. He basked in her success as a reflection of his own life, especially in politics. Both Frank and Katharine were sun-burst personalities. Everything and everyone in their orbit were lesser suns or smaller planets. That included Edith, the wife and mother. As Frank and Katharine's personas glowed ever brighter, Edith's light began to dim. Then, at age 54, she was diagnosed with breast cancer. By the time the cancer was caught, it had already metastasized. Edith's oncologist gave her a dire prognosis: 12-18 months. Until the cancer was discovered, Katharine had almost quit communicating with her mother. Edith was just so reticent about everything while Frank always boomed his approval about her slightest achievement. For the next few months after the cancer became terminal, both Frank and Katharine seemed in denial about Edith's situation. They never discussed it as a family. Edith had always been so quiet. However, she was still a steadying influence in their small family. Edith never complained about her condition. "She is so stoic," Katharine told her dad one day. Frank just nodded his head in agreement. Gradually, Edith began fading. Since she had never offered much of an opinion about anything, the quietness of her illness did not strike anyone as unusual. She was just there, as she always was. Until she was not. Edith made her transition exactly one year after the doctor gave her the fatal timeline. On the way back home after Edith's well-attended memorial service, Katharine was surprised that her father had burst into prolonged sobbing. It did not seem like him, she thought.

At first, everything seemed almost normal after her mom's passing. Not having Edith's quiet presence in her life did not seem much different to Katharine. Frank, however, seemed devastated over the loss of his wife. He began hanging out almost every night at his favorite bar. His daily and nightly texts and phone calls to Katharine became infrequent and then stopped altogether. Katharine felt as though she had lost both parents. She finally confronted her father over his sudden lack of interest in her life. Frank did not deny that he had quit doing the constant cheerleading for his only child. However, nothing changed. In fact, she virtually never heard from him anymore. Then six months after Edith's death, Frank announced that he was marrying LaVerne, a regular patron at the bar. Katharine was shocked beyond words. How could he do this to her?

"What about me?" she finally exploded at her father on the day of his wedding, "Who will pay attention to me?" "Oh Kat," he said, "You will find somebody. I just need a nice quiet woman like LaVerne to laugh at my jokes and drink with me at night and on weekends. I remember that you never talked to your mother very much. Just think of me as Edith."

THE SIXTH COMMANDMENT:

YOU SHALL NOT MURDER

The voices in Ted's brain were becoming insistent. They had been railing at him for weeks now. They just kept getting louder and more demanding. He did not try to silence them anymore. Their constant message never varied. It was always the same. Somebody needed to die before they would quit hounding him. Where did this angry cacophony of voices originate? None seemed familiar. The one thing that baffled Ted: they were all women. He had not spoken to his birth mother in years. His last foster mom had handed him to the state six months ago. His only sister was still swimming around somewhere in foster care, but he did not know where. Ted never had a real encounter with the opposite sex, much less an actual date. The girls at his schools all avoided him and scattered if he dared try to hang with them. Ted overheard one girl tell another: "That guy creeps me out." Stuck-up b-----s", he sneered to himself.

Ted was not bad looking. He stood exactly one inch over six feet and a guy in the school gym had once admired his build. Ted wondered if the boy was gay. Anyway, Ted just muttered something under his breath and stalked away. He avoided the gym after that.

Friends are not easy to come by when you were a kick-around foster child. Most of his relationships with families in the system had been brief. Changing schools frequently was an ongoing problem. Ted had been in four different high schools in the past three years. Although he never graduated, he did not plan on going back to school again anytime soon. Ted Bunton was having bigger challenges with the voices. They never explained why someone had to die before they would quit tormenting him. However, the chorus was clear that the victim had to be a woman. Ted had resisted the voices until now. Despite the unlucky cards that kept turning up in his life, he was not generally a violent person. He avoided confrontations. In fact, Ted had never struck anybody (male of female) in anger. However, he could be hard on animals. A stray cat or dog became unlucky the moment they crossed Ted's path.

The supernatural and insistent choir of voices had become so loud that Ted had to pay attention. To appease them, he began half-heartedly planning how the murder would take place. Perhaps he could stalk an unsuspecting girl at the local mall. She would need to be alone. Ted could follow his prey back to the parking lot and kidnap the victim while she was fumbling with her car keys. On one recent afternoon, he had loitered around the local mall until spotting a likely prospect. Just as he was about to make his move in the parking lot, the teen age girl's six foot-four tough-looking boyfriend came jogging up from another direction. The encounter could have been disastrous, Ted thought. He quickly slinked away. Then Ted had an epiphany. He recalled a picnic area at a nearby lake. There was an accessible bluff overlooking the lake where people (including women) went alone when craving solitude. He had visited the isolated site himself a few times when he was REALLY hating people. On a couple of occasions, Ted had observed young women at the bluff reading or just relaxing. Anyway, it might be worth checking it out.

The next afternoon, Ted rode his bicycle to the bluff. It was not a steep grade. He parked his bike at a small rest area and began walking around to the bluff. Sure enough, he came upon a little waterfall area, where a steady stream of water was emptying into lake. Lying on a blanket nearby was a somewhat older woman, probably in her early 30s. That was slightly older than what Ted had in mind, but it still looked like the perfect set-up. The angry voices were in full rant-form now, screaming "You must kill someone today." Ted walked up to where the woman was sitting. She had both knees propped up near her face. She appeared deep in thought and had not noticed him approaching. Good, he thought. He reached in his back pocket to make sure the screwdriver was in place. On the way up the path to the waterfall, he also had unearthed a decent size rock. He planned to knock his victim unconscious and then finish her off with the screwdriver. There was plenty of nearby brush where a body could be easily hidden. Things were falling into place. The woman suddenly looked up. She did not seem frightened by Ted's sudden appearance. Instead, she smiled sweetly. Perhaps she wants some company, he wondered as he drew closer. He saw that the woman had short blonde hair and hazel eyes. She was about five-six and slender, not like most of the hippos that slouched around the mall or paraded through the grocery store. Ted had worried that a stout woman or an athletic girl might be harder to subdue. This one looked perfect for what he had in mind.

"Hello," she smiled, "You are right on time." The comment disarmed Ted. A puzzled look spread across his face.

"Er, what do you mean, I'm right on time?"
"I was just looking at the waterfall while I waited for you," she said with a nod of her head. "it's quite relaxing. Won't you sit here with me for just a moment?"

This is a strange, Ted thought. I wonder if she might be unstable, you know, like having a mental problem. There were a lot of weirdos out there. You could not be too careful.

He did kneel half-way, but also positioned himself so that he could pounce on her when the time came for the kill.

"You seem more nervous than I expected," she said softly.

"What the hell do you mean, lady?" Ted asked in a snarly voice.

"We may as well get on with things," she said with unexpected brusqueness. "How were you planning to do it?"

"Do what?" Ted asked. The rock tucked underneath his shirt fell out and tumbled onto the ground.

"Oh, I see now," the woman said with a grin. "Not very original."

He tried to rise to a crouching position, but his body would not cooperate. He was frozen into place.

In a lightning move, the woman chopped Ted hard in the larynx with the edge of her right hand. The blow stunned the young man and he fell backward while grabbing his throat. With a quick motion, she reached down and seized the rock that Ted had planned to use on her. She slammed it hard twice into his right temple, killing him.

She stood over his dead body for a few seconds and then dropped an old newspaper on his bloody chest.

The headline read: "Second Woman Murdered at Waterfall by Serial Killer."

The woman glanced down at Ted's crumpled body before she smiled and disappeared slowly into the ethers.

The newspaper was dated exactly 50 years ago today. Underneath the headline was a photograph of the killer's latest victim. She was a slender, blonde woman with short hair.

THE SEVENTH COMMANDMENT:

THOU SHALT NOT COMMIT ADULTERY

Pastor Jim was looking forward to his new job as interim minister at the iconic church in Surprise, Arizona. It was an older, but wealthy community, located about 20 miles northwest of Phoenix. Many retirees, especially from the Midwest, had swarmed into the area located near Sun City and Sun City West. They embraced Surprise as a desert oasis in their later years. These people were the cream of the cream for oldsters. They were rich enough to enjoy comfortable retirements through their accumulation of wealth. Money is like a protective balm for the aging skin, Pastor Jim thought.

Not that he was that young anymore, Jim sighed. He thought about his 65th birthday party only six months ago. He had not been especially happy to retire as the assistant minister for his megachurch in the Chicago suburbs. But the lay board wanted younger blood—and to replace him with a female minister. Jim thought about resisting the pressure to retire, but then decided not to fight it. No use fighting progress, he thought. Jim left graciously in a peaceful manner and burned no bridges. One of his former congregants had retired to the Valley of the Sun some years ago. When he learned of Pastor Jim's retirement, it seemed natural that the Chicagoland minister would make an excellent interim until a new pastor or husband/wife team might be secured. Everything flowed in divine order and Jim was hired by the church at a decent salary. Although not near what he had been earning, it still represented an excellent supplement to his retirement package from the megachurch.

Jim knew the Arizona congregation was well-endowed. Just two years before, three separate widows had all died within a 60-day period. Strangely enough, each had left similar bequests to the church. All three legacies were in the amount of $800,000 each. The church was already mortgage free and now had more than $1,500,000 in money market securities. Considering that most churches had no huge cushions, this represented a dream position from any new minister's standpoint.

During his first week on the new job, the church's board of directors held a special lunch for their new pastor. Of course, they all wanted to know about Jim's wife. She had been at the church only once, during his formal interview for the job. Margaret, his wife of 35 years, was still back at home in South Barrington, wrapping up the sale of their house. She planned to move out to Arizona, just as soon as it closed. At the board lunch, many pleasantries were passed. Louella Munson, the 75-year young board president, was quite generous with her praise of the new interim minister.

"We're very lucky to have found such a young and vibrant leader," Louella beamed. Pastor Jim felt a bit uncomfortable with her description as he was only 10 years Louella's junior. However, she was an outspoken, powerful and dominating presence. She looked and acted much younger than Jim in many ways. Her form-fitting dresses at the Sunday services always drew eye-rolling from the choir and whispered comments from the front row of 90-somethings. Louella's husband, "Mr. Bob" Sanders, was a wealthy Ohioan. He had just turned 93 and been absent from church for nearly three months. Louella had been Mr. Sanders former secretary at his successful auto parts chain. When the original Mrs. Sanders had passed away 20 years before, Louella and her boss quickly became betrothed. They eventually retired and made the move to Arizona, leaving "Mr. Bob's" two sons in charge of the company.

When the church board meeting ended, Louella asked if she might have a word with Pastor Jim. He agreed but wondered about its purpose. She took a quick seat on the office couch and patted the cushion for Jim to join her. Louella was dressed in a typical Arizona white cashmere sweater, flowery blouse and light tan slacks. She also sported a colorful scarf tossed loosely around her neck. As Jim seated himself on the couch, Louella lifted herself up and plopped down even closer to him. Now they were only a couple of inches apart.

The hair on the back of Jim's neck jumped to immediate attention.

"Uh, oh," he thought, "Is she coming on to me?"

"Now Jim," Louella said in a lowered voice, "Don't be shy. I can't help it if I find you attractive in a non-churchy sort of way." Then, she reached over and gently touched him on the upper leg. It was a fleeting probe and did not linger. However, her dreamy smile was a definite invitation to something other than Southwestern friendliness.

"I think you and I are going to get along fine," she said, looking directly into his eyes. Jim felt a chill spiral through his body.

"Er, I'm not sure what you mean, Louella," he managed in a rather meek voice. Jim knew his response did not rise to anything close to vibrant.

"Oh, I think you do, Jimmy. I want to spend some time with you."

"No, I really don't," the pastor said as he shifted his body slightly away from her. "I hope that I have not misled you in some way. I am not sure what you mean, but Margaret and I are happily married. She will be out here soon."

"Oh, I was hoping that you and I would have time to get acquainted before she arrives. In fact, after church on Sunday, I am planning to leave for our cabin on Lake Havasu. I would be honored if you could join me. We can have a mini-board retreat, just the two of us. I really want you to see the Lake. You and Margaret can use the house anytime you want." "Will "Mr. Bob" be there?" Pastor Jim asked, already knowing the answer.

"Oh no, honey," Louella answered. "Old Bob is on his last legs. He rarely leaves the house anymore. I hope you will consider my offer. Do you water ski? Are you into that? I can let you drive our boat. We have a nice 35-footer." "Nope, I'm not into the water stuff," Jim said, firmly shutting that door on that possibility.

"Say, Louella, can you excuse me, I have some notes to prepare for my talk on Sunday."

After the board president departed in a semi-huff, Pastor Jim opened his desk drawer. He found a sheet of church stationery and placed it in front of him. Before he could think more about it, he hand-wrote his resignation letter. It was effective immediately.

Then, Jim texted Margaret and told her to forget about closing on the house in Illinois. He would be back home soon and explain everything.

THE EIGHTH COMMANDMENT:

YOU SHALL NOT STEAL

Amy Thurman had never meant to steal from the company. It all began, as most illegal schemes do, innocently and without forethought or malice. Her employer was a medium-size hardware retailer. The founding father had begun the now 22-store chain selling wrenches and nuts and bolts out of his detached garage. There were only three stores open when the founder died 15 years ago. The second generation, consisting of his two sons and daughter, had methodically expanded the firm. The trio would watch for new suburban communities opening near their hub city.

They would swoop in, buy some still-cheap property and be the first hardware store to open. New homeowners typically need more hardware items, so the plan was a natural and immediately successful. The "Barton Family Hardware Store" was now projected to open two new stores every year for the foreseeable future. Sales and profits kept rising. Amy had started working for the Barton family three years ago. She had received her degree in accounting from the state university and was looking for a job. One day, as she scanned the online job postings, Amy spotted an opening for an assistant bookkeeper at the Barton hardware stores. She applied immediately, hit it off with the founder's three children and landed the job. For the past three years, she had been the primary assistant to 70-something Tom Downey, the firm's chief accountant and treasurer. Tom had been with the founder almost from the beginning of the company. The Barton siblings liked the aging Mr. Downey, but he was a dinosaur when it came to digital knowledge. Amy was a whiz at the new technology. It was not long before Tom Downey had been given a nice dinner and exceptionally generous retirement package. He was now living on his newly purchased small yacht somewhere in the Caribbean. Amy had taken over his old position without any drama. The Barton children quickly named the young woman as vice-pres-

ident and treasurer for financial affairs. Her
future looked bright indeed.

When a new Indian casino opened near one of
their stores, the Barton's were invited to
attend the Grand Opening. They were busy,
so Amy was asked to represent them. She
went and was thunderstruck at the glitz and
dynamic feel of the casino. Amy had never
been a gambler. Her experience inside the
gaming world was almost non-existent. Her
father's alcoholism and the family money
problems made the young woman even more
wary of risk.

When the Grand Opening ended, Amy had
stayed to explore this exciting new attraction.
One of the casino managers escorted her
around, pointing out the different machines
and tables. She was drawn to the slot
machines. One of the $5 machines was open.
The casino manager invited Amy to take a
seat in front of the flashy machine and try her
luck. He gave the young woman $100 in $5
coins and then excused himself. Amy had
finally peeled herself away four hours later.
She could not get enough of the instant rush
every time she pulled the handle down. The
instant gratification of a winning spin, or the
quick dejection when she lost, thrilled her
beyond belief. When Amy cashed in her coins
at the end of the four-hour high, she received
a check from the casino for $2,850. She felt

giddy and strangely fulfilled. Her life had changed forever.

Amy stayed away from the bright lights and the spinning cherries for a full 10 days. But the parable of a moth to a flame became true for her. At first, she limited most her gambling to Friday and Saturday nights. She soon found that after 3 p.m. on Fridays, her work mind shut down and her gambling brain became engaged. Amy usually arrived at her perch in front of the $5 machine by 6 p.m. on Fridays. She did feel some pride in that she could walk away at 11 p.m. Of course, she knew that the remainder of the weekend would start at noon on Saturday. She always had lunch first before sitting down at her machine. She usually closed things down at the Midnight buffet. Amy rarely drank and never smoked while gambling. Those distractions slowed her down. Of course, casino management already had Amy in their sights. They had spoken to her on two occasions, both times when her debt had exceeded $10,000. But she always had the money before the next weekend arrived. The casino managers backed off, but they did consider recommending that Amy get help for what had become an obvious addiction. They decided to let it go for now, with a thought to review things again in six months. When her debt had creeped up to $15,000, she was summoned to the casino manager's office. He said they were thinking about banning her from the machines. Amy pleaded with the managers for one more chance. She had cried and they relented, at least for now. Again, there was no follow up. Her first real embezzlement came to cover a $20,000 debt. It had been easy beyond belief. Amy established a fake vendor account, using false information that included billing invoices. She would simply issue a company check to cover the fake invoice. Amy knew the Barton company was audited annually by an outside professional accounting firm. Her intention was to fully repay every bit of the money before the audit took place. However, she was never able to cover the debt. It was now approaching six figures.

It took her a few weeks, but she finally manu-factured two separate sets of company books. One was real, the other fake. When the audit came, the correct books would be handed to the auditor. Amy secured a hefty personal loan using her retirement account as collat-eral and then maxxed out three of her credit cards to make sure the bank records matched. I should be good to go, she thought. She then locked the fake corporate books in the trunk of her car.

Everything progressed well, until one Friday night her car was stolen from the casino parking lot. Of course, Amy was frantic. The car was not recovered during the weekend. However, when she had arrived at work on Monday, the office receptionist notified her that the Barton family was waiting in the board room. When Amy arrived, the two brothers and sister were seated with the company attorney and two officials from the outside auditing company.

It turned out that her stolen vehicle had been dropped off at the oldest brother's home on Saturday afternoon. The false set of company books were on the front seat, along with a note. It had read: "Hey Barton Hardware. Looks like somebody is cooking your books. We thought you might want to know." It was signed: "The Dudley Do-Rights".

Amy never discovered the "Dudley Do-Rights" real identity. She pleaded guilty and served a four-year sentence, with six months off for good behavior. After she became free, it was back to searching the on-line classifieds. Surely some fine family company needed an experienced bookkeeper. Amy knew just the person.

THE NINTH COMMANDMENT:

YOU SHALL NOT BEAR FALSE WITNESS

Billy Patterson wanted a male chum. At 17 and a junior in high school, he had experienced only two best friends in his young life. Johnny Harris had been his close bud in elementary school, but then Johnny moved to another state when his dad's job was transferred. In the seventh grade, Billy and Buddy Crenshaw had connected through a love of video games. They spent hours together, playing away. When Billy headed to high school two years ago, Buddy's father had suddenly retired from the military and the entire family moved to Hawaii. Billy was without a best friend again.

Billy did not crave a huge collection of friends. One suited him perfectly. A simple replacement for Johnny and Buddy was his goal. Billy's locker at high school was located next to a new kid in school, a dude named Todd. He and Todd had exchanged some friendly banter during the first weeks of the fall term. The new boy smiled a lot and never seemed to arrive at school moody or bad-tempered. Billy liked Todd's even disposition. His own home was an unstable place. Both of his parents drank every day. If Billy's dad arrived home from work in a good mood, then his mom would be smashed. On other days, things happened in reverse. Weekends were the worst. By Sunday night, both of his parents had consumed copious amounts of beer and wine.

They were usually in bed shortly after sun-
down. Neither one allowed much time for
Billy.

Nor was his sister Michelle much help. "Shell"
was the flip side of her brother. She had scads
of friends, far too many in Billy's opinion. His
sister was never free from her cell phone. It
was constantly binging off with texts from
another friend wanting to talk. Billy was lone-
some. He had gotten up his nerve to invite
Todd over for some gaming, when something
alarming took place. Billy and Todd were
standing near their lockers chatting when a
third boy appeared. "Charlie" stopped by to
greet Todd. He barely acknowledged Billy.
The conversation quickly became two sided
with Billy being the odd man out. As Billy
turned to head for study hall, he heard Todd
invite Charlie over to hang out after school.
For hours afterward, Billy obsessed about his
new competitor for Todd's attention. He felt
rejected and abandoned. It was an all too
familiar feeling. The next day, he decided on a
strategy. It was his only hope. Billy would
turn Todd and Charlie against each other.
How? By spreading falsehoods, that is how.
He had no other option.

Billy began his plot by casually mentioning to
Todd a comment he claimed to have overheard. Billy said his sister had been talking to

one of her friends. The friend knew Charlie, but not Todd. Billy quoted his sister as saying: "My friend Andrea knows Charlie," Shel had supposedly said, "He really does not like your locker mate Todd. He called him a dork." When Billy repeated the comment to Todd, a look of hurt and bewilderment flashed across the other teenager's face. "I thought Charlie and I were friends," he mumbled as he slinked off. Billy had drawn first blood.

His plot kept unfolding. Billy mentioned to Charlie that Todd did not want to hang out with him after school. "But he feels sorry for you," Billy added. "He doesn't think you have any friends." A hurt and pained look crossed Charlie's face. Billy had scored another point against Todd and Charlie's friendship. This kept on for a while. Todd and Charlie quickly cooled on each other. Now, Billy had more options. He could choose either Todd or Charlie as a best friend. He could tell Charlie appreciated the "head's up" on Todd's supposed duplicity. It had forged a new bond between them.

Billy did not feel badly about spreading his lies. He was in survival mode, both at home and school. He was only doing what he had to do. If someone else got hurt in the process, so be it. Things changed one day after school. The car that Todd was driving got T-boned by a drunk driver. The teenager was rushed to the ICU in extremely critical condition. Word spread throughout the student body that Todd might not survive. His kidneys were damaged beyond repair. The next day at school, the principal announced that Todd's family was looking for a donor. To everyone's surprise, Charlie was the first to volunteer. He offered one of his kidneys as a replacement. The two teenagers were a perfect match. The operation was scheduled and performed right away. To everyone's relief, Todd would be OK. Charlie suddenly became the school hero.

As for Billy, he became accustomed again to playing his video games alone. He also vowed to never tell another lie. And he did not. Then one day, he was standing at his locker when Charlie and Todd strolled up. "Hey, Billy," Charlie said, "Todd and I were wondering if you would like to hang out after school." Billy quickly accepted the invitation. By their time senior year was finished, everyone in school was calling Billy, Todd, and Charlie "The Three Amigos."

THE TENTH COMMANDMENT:

YOU SHALL NOT COVET

Margie Lambert and Kitten Kelley had lived next door to each other for six years in

Duluth, GA, a wealthy area located 22 miles northeast of Atlanta. Margie was a stay-at-home mom with daughter Kimberly (14) and sons Robert Lambert III (12) and Thomas (10). Kit was a residential real estate superstar, specializing in high end properties in the Gwinnett County area.

Robert Lambert, Jr. was Margie's husband of 16 years. Robbie had turned 40 on his last birthday. He was an attorney for Georgia Power, the largest subsidiary of the Southern Company. Robbie had progressed up the corporate ladder unimpeded. He was now assistant general counsel for the utility company, earning $250K per year.

Eddy Kelley was Kit's husband. He also had recently hit "The Big 4-0". Eddy had tried several jobs before finding a home as assistant manager at the Valvoline Instant Oil Change station 1.7 miles from the Kelley home. Eddy usually ate a quick lunch at home by himself as Kit had at least one and often multiple showings every day. Kit was the big breadwinner in the family. Her commissions for the prior year had totaled $305,000. Although the pandemic had thrown the current year off a bit, residential real estate was still exploding in the Metro.

Exodus 20

Eddy was home for lunch, pulled up to his
high-top kitchen counter. He was chowing
down on a hand-made turkey sandwich
when he heard a knock at his back door.
Eddy and Kit had no children, so it could not
be a neighborhood kid coming or going. Eddy
peered around the corner and saw Margie
Lambert waiting for a response. She was in
a stylish white tennis dress and carrying her
favorite racket. Eddy just stared at her for a
few seconds. He had long ago decided that
Marg had the best female legs in the neighborhood. Her dark hair and fresh-faced look
completed the All-American package. She
could have been in her early 30s, but Eddy
knew Margie would be celebrating her 40th
birthday at a cookout on his back porch in a
few days.

"Come on in," Eddy called out. "But Kit's not
home right now. She had a showing this
afternoon."

"I figured," Marg answered, "I didn't see her
Escalade." She walked straight to the counter and positioned herself almost a little too
close at Eddy's right elbow. "But I really
wanted to visit with you. I saw your truck
pull in the driveway."

"Oh yeah, what about?" Eddy inquired, feeling some wariness.

"I was wondering if we could bring anything to the party on Saturday?"

"Nope," Eddy said, putting down his sandwich. "Kit's got everything under control, just like always. All you and Rob need to do is show up."

"Your wife is truly amazing," Margie smiled. "You know, she is my hero. There are plenty of other women in the neighborhood who feel the same way about her. You're really a luck guy, Eddy."

"How well I know it," he responded with a smile. "Because of her, I can do all of the weekend hunting and fishing that I want. I am getting lots of time alone at our new cabin up in Blairsville. Your Rob was there a couple of weekends ago. You will have to come up with him some time."

"Yes, I remembered Rob has already been there," Margie said, "But you know these kids. Something is happening every weekend."

"Yeah, I know," Eddy replied with a downward glance toward the floor. He and Kit had tried to have children for a few years with no success. When her real estate career began soaring, baby discussions disappeared.

"Anyway, I've got something more serious than the party to discuss," Marg said, with an unexpected frown.

"Shoot," Eddy grinned.

"There is no other way to say this, Eddy. I'm in love with your wife."

Eddy Kelley looked dumbstruck.

"What did you just say?"

"I said that I am in love with Kit. And she loves me. We care about each other. I thought you should know."

Eddy just stared at his neighbor.

"Cut the BS, Marg!" he said, raising his voice.

"It's true," Marg smiled, "I love everything about her. She is the most perfect person I know. I have never met anyone like her. The great personality, the long red hair, the flashy car, the clothes. I just love everything about her."

"You don't know what you are saying, Marg. Are you drunk?"

"Yes," Margie answered, "I'm drunk on love for Kit. I had to tell you."

"I think you need to leave right now," Eddy said.

"I will go, but Kit and I want to schedule a time to sit down with you."

"Marg, you have three kids. I have no idea what has gotten into you, but you are not thinking straight."

"No," Marg said with a crooked grin, "Eddy, we are talking about real love."

Suddenly, Eddy's body stiffened.

"Wait a minute," he said, "I know what this is all about. Pretty clever, I must say."

"What do you mean?" Marg asked.

"Now, I understand," Eddy replied. "You and Kit think you are being cool."

"Why, whatever are you talking about Eddy Kelley?"

"Did Rob tell you what happened when we were at the cabin in Blairsville? That is what we are talking about here, isn't it?"

"Do you mean when you two crazy guys were drinking tequila and let your clothes fall off? Then you both jumped into the hot tub and made some whoopee?"

"It will never happen again, Margie. I promise."

"You bet it won't," Marg Lambert said, smashing her tennis racket hard on the kitchen counter. "Or Kit and I will bounce both of your sorry butts out on the pavement. Got it?"

Without a doubt, Eddy Kelley got it.

JESUS' TWO GREAT COMMANDMENTS

Besides the Ten Commandments in the Old Testament, Jesus also affirmed two great precepts in the New Testament. In Luke 10: 25, an "expert in the law" asked the Master: "Teacher, what must I do to inherit eternal life?" "What is written in the law," Jesus responded, "How do you read it?" The lawyer answered: "Love the Lord your God with all your heart and with all your soul and with all your strength and with all your mind and love your neighbor as yourself." To which Jesus replied: "You have answered correctly. Do this and you will live." Then Jesus proceeded to tell the story of "The Good Samaritan" as an example of caring for other people.

Without question, these two New Testament commandments represent crucial spiritual principles. "Loving your neighbor as yourself" is another way to affirm the Golden Rule: "Do unto others as you would have them do unto you." If this commandment was practiced by everyone, human relationships would improve dramatically. "Love the Lord with every bit of your heart, soul, strength and mind" would establish humankind on the perfect spiritual path. These "commandments" recognize how human beings are susceptible to forgetting God and getting caught up with their own idols.

It perhaps could be argued that Jesus' twin commandments offer a softer and more gentle approach to guiding human behavior. However, that does not diminish their direct power in telling people (a) to consciously put God first in every area of their lives and (b) to equate others at the same level as themselves. In the latter precept, Jesus takes on the innate desire of the ego to control our human emotions. By default, most people cooperate with the ego and put themselves first. It illustrates the average person's obsession with "self".

By focusing on these two paths to eternal life, Jesus wants to lift us to a higher perspective. Loving God with every fiber of our being and equating others with ourselves serve as the hidden secrets of human life.

THE TWELVE GIFTS OF THE TEN COMMANDMENTS

1. THE GIFT OF LOVE—If God had not loved the Jewish people so much, He would not have cared about their behavior. He wanted them to live the best and most disciplined lives possible. God knew that happens when we operate from our highest consciousness. Instead of abandoning the freed slaves to their own devices, God provided the ten specific laws that would guarantee a more trouble-free life. He was telling them: "Follow My Laws completely and you can maximize your freedom."

2. THE GIFT OF INVOLVEMENT—God wanted intimate involvement in the lives of His chosen people. They needed to feel His concern about their behavior. God does not function as an absentee parent. When it comes to paying attention to our words, thoughts and actions, God always stays tuned in. He knows everything

about us at every moment. Spirit is not out to catch or punish us. He wants all His sheep to remain safe and secure in the flock.

3. THE GIFT OF CLARITY—Each of The Ten Commandments leaves no doubt about what God expects. There is nothing wishy-washy about any of the ten precepts. There are no addendums or caveats. For example, the Eighth Commandment clearly states: "You shall not steal". It does not add a disclaimer, such as: "Unless of course you really, really need what you are about to steal." God says what He means and means what He says.

4. THE GIFT OF EXPECTATION—The LORD expects the Jewish people to follow His Ten Commandments. Spirit honors them by creating an expectation of obedience. God also hopes they will create aspirations for themselves. They should want to live in alignment with the higher principles.

5. THE GIFT OF DISCIPLINE—God understood that living a life of discipline would be hard for the ex-slaves. It is always uncomfortable correcting errant

behavior. Personal change requires courage and determination. Saying "no" to the prevailing culture requires un-common dedication and strength of character. The Commandments codify the new norms of behavior expected by God. But He appreciates the challenge.

6. THE GIFT OF WISDOM—God care-fully considered these divine laws be-fore designating them as official commandments. There is deep spiritual wisdom contained in each of the pre-cepts. God wants the Jewish people to see Him as the sacred fountain of all knowledge. We too are blessed with these Truths that light our spiritual path. The eternal wisdom contained in God's Ten Commandments guarantees a deeper and more fulfilled life for us all.

7. THE GIFT OF GOODNESS—God wants only "good" for the beloved chil-dren of Israel. The Ten Command-ments are rife with goodness. They emphasize honesty, considerate treat-ment of others and an unwavering fo-cus on NOT doing certain things that might create trouble. When positive behavior becomes second nature, we all

reap the bountiful harvest that comes from practicing spiritual principles.

8. THE GIFT OF BOUNDARIES—Many people grow up without any knowledge of boundaries. Having and adhering to strong boundaries can change anyone's life for the better. However, boundary crossers are everywhere. They live within most every family, school and workplace. They wait in the ready to test someone's defenses. With these ten major laws, God is defining good spiritual boundaries that can work for all human beings.

9. THE GIFT OF PRINCIPLES—God desires that all humankind live by spiritual principles. Traversing our life journey steeped in God's laws offers the best path toward peace and fulfillment. Anyone can sink to the bottom of a meaningless abyss by following an unprincipled life. God designed the Ten Commandments for those wandering in a moral desert. Sprit hopes human beings choose timeless principles over our own ego-driven wishes.

10. THE GIFT OF DIRECTION—Spirit sent Moses' followers a definite signal

on which route to take for religious deliverance. God did not expect the former slaves to make good decisions about their own behavior. The Ten Commandments address negative tendencies and offers specific solutions. God wants us to stay on the correct Path. When we follow His spiritual direction, we stay focused, safe and untroubled.

11. THE GIFT OF UNDERSTANDING---
God understood the freed slaves. He created every one of them, just as He has created each of us. Before you and I were born into the physical world, the LORD knew our every strength and talent, vulnerability and weakness. Spirit then equipped us with the needed resources. When you and I adhere to God's plan for our destiny, we can be a light to everyone that crosses our path.

12. THE GIFT OF PROTECTION—If we broke any of the Ten Commandments, we could be putting ourselves and others at risk. God wants us to remain safe throughout our earthly journey. Doing anything that might jeopardize our or someone else's safety flies against God's divine plan. We should all seek to

complete our human lives as smoothly as possible. God gave us these ten specific laws as guidelines for good behavior. Following them provides us with a celestial insurance policy.

A FINAL THOUGHT

Are the Ten Commandments the best rem-
edy to counteract the world's descent into
immorality and negative behavior? Taken by
themselves, these historical precepts cannot
overnight counteract generations of bad
words and actions. However, a new focus on
their eternal wisdom might act to stop the
current slide. Before we can reverse any negative trend, we must halt its momentum.
Human beings can be stubborn when anyone
demands anything new from them. Unless
people want to change their ways, nothing
will happen. The mesmerism of the media-
driven material world remains powerful. Our
obsession with technology seems more likely
to proceed unabated. No matter what God
might want for us, making societal changes
is hard. Maybe if human beings would simply become more aware of the Ten Commandments, the conversation about a new
direction could begin. One can only hope and
pray for the wisdom required to embrace
God's divine laws.

THE END

ABOUT THE AUTHOR

Rev. Allen C. Liles is a graduate of Baylor
University in Waco, TX and The Unity
School of Religious Studies at Unity Village,
MO. Before being ordained as a non-denomi-
national minister in 1993, he served as the
vice-president for public relations at The
Southland Corporation (7-Eleven Stores) in
Dallas, TX. and communications manager for
The McLane Company in Temple, TX. Rev.
Liles was also Senior Director for Outreach
at Unity Village 1995-2001 and senior minister for Unity Churches in Missouri, Arizona
and Minnesota. He is the originator and
author of the new "Classic Bible Chapters"
series.

BOOKS BY ALLEN C. LILES

Ephesians 6: Putting On the Full Armor of God

John 14: The Most Important Chapter in the New Testament

Sitting With God/Meditating for God's Divine Guidance

The 7 Puzzles of Life/God's Plan to Save the World

The Forever Penny/How Our Loved Ones Stay Connected After Death

Oh Thank Heaven/The Story of the Southland Corporation

E-Books on www.smashwords.com

The 12 Promises of Heaven

Friends of Jesus

E-Spiritual Rehab

The Book of Celeste/God Recruits a Blogger

The Book of Floyd/God Transforms a Racist

The Book of Ethan/God Confronts Teen Suicide

www.ingramcontent.com/pod-product-compliance
Lightning Source LLC
Chambersburg PA
CBHW060946040426
42445CB00011B/1020